D1126605

INTERNATIONAL THEATRE AND CINEMA

EDITED BY HERBERT MARSHALL

THE CHINESE THEATRE

JACK CHEN

THE CHINESE THEATRE

ILLUSTRATED BY THE AUTHOR

London

DENNIS DOBSON LTD

First published in Great Britain in MCMXLIX by DENNIS DOBSON
LTD, 12 Park Place, St James's, London SW1. All rights reserved.
Printed in Great Britain by THE BOWERING PRESS, Plymouth.

165-/R

CONTENTS

To the Memory of
LU HSUN

INTRODUCTION

THERE ARE THREE main types of theatre art in China today. All of them have enthusiastic audiences.

Firstly, there is the Classical Theatre. This is still the most widespread. It is popular among all classes, all over the country. With its characteristic theatre buildings, its ties with religious ritual, its highly stylised conventions of staging, acting, costume and elocution, its historical or mythological subject-matter, it draws its main inspiration from the ancient theatrical tradition and thought of the Chinese people. It is essentially a feudal, medieval theatrical tradition carried over into modern times.

Secondly, there is the Western Style Theatre. This was originally inspired by the theatrical tradition of Western countries as received via Japan. It has grown up during the last thirty years with the growth of the modern urban classes of China and their intelligentsia.

Though it still draws its main inspiration and most of its plays from the classical and modern theatrical culture of the West, it is by no means a mere copy. It now has its own native dramatists, its own talented cadres of actors, its own producers. It can present mature interpretations of Molière, Shakespeare, Gogol or Shaw. It is influenced by the ancient dramatic tradition of China but its dramaturgy deals almost exclusively with modern themes and problems from a realistic standpoint. Its popularity is in the big cities.

Thirdly, there is the Yangko Theatre. This is the most recent in development. It originated only during the last ten years in the Communist-led Liberated Areas of China. It is a theatre of the revolutionary movement and spreads as the democratic revolution led by the working class, spreads over the country.

Introduction

Many revolutionary intellectuals from the urban centres sought to put their knowledge and talent at the disposal of the Communist-led, anti-Japanese guerilla Resistance Movement during the 1931–45 Japanese invasion of China. They found that Western style drama had but a limited attraction for the peasants who form 80 per cent of the Chinese people and who were the backbone of the Resistance Movement as they are now a main force of the revolutionary democratic movement. The Classical Theatre, though popular with the people, was found to be too deeply steeped in convention, too hardened in form to be a suitable medium for a new, popular democratic and revolutionary message. The intellectuals then sought and found inspiration in the still living and vital folk art tradition of the people—the Yangko folk dance drama of Shensi Province—which, indeed, was at an earlier date one of the sources of the Classical Theatre itself. The modern revolutionary intellectuals with the eager co-operation and encouragement of the people's own folk artists, musicians, dancers and performers, have made a synthesis of Yangko art, with adaptations of the Classical Theatre and of the modern Western Style Theatre to create the still evolving Yangko Theatre. This is a modern folk art theatre imbued with the most modern and revolutionary ideas of world culture. It is a new synthesis of Chinese and Western culture.

The Western Style Theatre is essentially a product of the urban middle class intellectuals. The Yangko Theatre is a product of the revolutionary alliance between the modern intellectuals and the peasantry—the inexhaustible source of China's vitality and strength and eternal renewal.

LONDON
June 15th, 1948

CHAPTER ONE

THE
CLASSICAL
THEATRE

THE TIME IS the present. We are walking along the unpaved, trampled mud streets of Ninghsia, capital of the province of that name, a typical old Chinese town of the historic North-west. Over the roofs we see the crenellated city wall, the drum tower over the gate with its up-curved pointed eaves and roof figures of gods and dragons. The open-fronted shops display their goods: there are rich silks and humble cottons; there are cases of ivory figures and tasselled silverware. A mysterious herb-shop sells snake skin remedies and aphrodisiac *gin seng* roots with queerly contorted human looking shapes. But next door is a cyclists' shop and next to that a Chinese 'Woolworths' cluttered with cheap shoes, electric torches, thermos flasks, gaudy cotton textiles and cheap oleograph prints of bathing beauties.

From many yards away we hear the clash of cymbals and the wailing note of the *Hu Ch'in* violin, the steady wooden 'clap-clap' of the time-beater. The high trembling falsetto of an actor . . . but it is drowned momentarily by the hum of a single high-flying mail plane.

A lady of the streets turns down a side lane. She wears a close-fitting gown of emerald green satin. Her tightly drawn-back hair glistens with aromatic oils. Her long 'pig-tail' is bound at its end with scarlet thread. Her socks are rich shell pink. Her shoes are of white satin, embroidered with vermilion flowers. Her face is thickly powdered white with two bright spots of colour on her cheeks shaded by a saucy fringe. Her amah, soberly garbed in black silk coatee and trousers, totters along on her tiny bound feet, carrying a lute.

The weather-worn triumphal wooden arch has long since shed its brilliant red and green paint. The gold inscribed name-board over the gate is tarnished. The green posters giving the programme and the actors' names are written in flowing black ink by hand. The vestibule, like everything else about the theatre building is in a state of the utmost delapidation. The unpainted woodwork has turned dingy grey streaked with black. All around the wall and pilasters are greasy black marks from countless hands and waiting backs. The crimson, emerald green and black and white frieze of good-luck signs and flowers is cobwebbed and stained. Once they have built a building, the old style provincials seem satisfied to allow it to settle comfortably into decay until the time comes to build anew.

At small cost, we enter the auditorium. It holds about six to seven hundred people on the ground floor and in the gallery that runs around three sides. It is fairly full although it is just after six in the afternoon and the plays continue till after ten.

The stage is like the Elizabethan stage—almost square and about five feet in height. At each side is a red lacquered column some 20 feet high, supporting a canopy. Each carries a black oblong panel with appropriate poetic inscriptions in gilded letters. The stage itself is railed in with a low balustrade, but this does not prevent several small urchins from sitting along its sides and dangling their feet over the edge.

The roof of the playhouse is sloped in two sections over heavy beams with a row of windows between. These light the hall during the day. Four huge acetylene lamps over and before the stage provide lighting at night. There are no spotlights or limelights.

Square tables and chairs occupy half of the floor space in front of the stage. These are the most expensive seats. Some wealthy merchants are already there, drinking tea, eating sweet cakes and fruit as they listen to the actors or discourse among themselves. Further back, the benches have little ledges behind their backs (like flat prayer-book rests on church pews) where teapots and edibles can be placed by less affluent spectators. The cheapest seats are on narrow benches on the sides of the stage. The gallery is divided into boxes. In the old days these used to be reserved for women only, but now this division of the sexes is no longer enforced. Except for the satin coatees of the merchants in the front seats, the blues and blacks and greys of Chinese cotton everyday wear predominate. Here and there is a soldier's khaki.

Startling is the contrast of the blaze of colour from the stage. It is carpeted with a deep blue Peking rug. The wall at the back is covered by a gorgeous silk curtain embroidered in peach and plum blossoms, phœnixes and clouds. On either side is a door-space also covered by smaller curtains in the same design. On the stage the actors' clothes are rich and brilliant too. Even those representing poor people are garbed in silk and satin. As the importance of the plays or the actors increases towards the later evening, this beauty of costume is correspondingly heightened. There are no changes of scenery, but chairs and tables are covered with equally exquisite embroideries to match the costumes and the canopies that are carried in to represent tents, or beds, or the flags that represent rivers or armies.

On the left of the stage is the orchestra. The musicians are in street clothes and look shabby and somewhat bored, incongruous contrast to the brilliance of the actors. There is no visible leader, but the man with the wooden clapper beats a steady time, punctuating recitatives, or the rhythm of dances. There are cymbals, drums, gongs, trumpets, flutes, the plaintive *Hu Ch'in*. Several attendants stand unobtrusively on the side of the stage in their workaday clothes. It is a warm day and in keeping with the air of general unconcerned lack of ceremony, one wears no vest or shirt under his cotton jacket which is left comfortably unbuttoned. A large teapot in a cotton padded wickerwork cozy stands next to the stage column in full view of the audience.

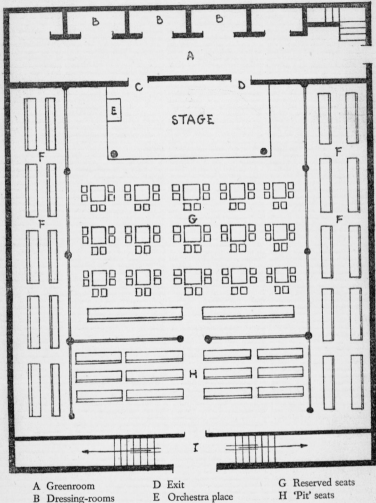

A Greenroom	D Exit	G Reserved seats
B Dressing-rooms	E Orchestra place	H 'Pit' seats
C Entrance	F Side seats	

As we take our seats at a table a pair of comedians are ending their act. One is a Mandarin with puffy side whiskers and stupid rouged cheeks. The other is a strange looking character in a voluminous gown with a white butterfly shaped smudge over his nose and eyes. He carries an umbrella and is busily selling a huge gold brick to the Mandarin. It is a back-chat dialogue with many loud 'asides' to the audience and much slap-stick. Every time the comic falls to the ground the drums give a loud 'boomp', quite in the style of the London Palladium.

As we settle ourselves more comfortably, an attendant brings us our pot of tea and little saucers of dried water-melon seeds. We crack them with our teeth, suck the sweet seed out and then, like everyone else, throw the husk away on the ground. We eat oranges and sticky cakes. To clean our hands and refresh ourselves we receive steaming, perfumed towels. The towel-boy on the side aisles throws these in hot bundles over the heads of the audience and our own table attendant catches them with unerring agility. No one takes any notice of this for it is going on in one or the other part of the hall the whole evening, except during especially exciting battle scenes or fine arias when the whole auditorium is in wrapt attention.

The next play is a real play, not just a dialogue, but it is still a comedy. A sing-song girl has been arrested and is brought before a pompous magistrate who speaks unctuously and hypocritically about morality. The girl, however, is more than a match for him. She tells how she was first ruined by a fellow who promised her all sorts of fine things. Who was this despicable cad, asks the magistrate, threatening him with fire and brimstone. 'He is here now, Your Honour!' replies the girl. 'Point him out', commands the magistrate and the maid points straight at the Bench. Exit magistrate with a complete loss of face. Case dismissed!

The maid is beautiful, vivacious, graceful. It is difficult to believe that 'she' is a young actor. Women have only recently been permitted by public opinion and the law to return to the stage. For many years previously the only exception to the all-male theatre was one in Shanghai formed entirely of women and known as the 'Theatre of Cats'.

China has never—till very recent years—been worried by the pros and cons of 'art for art's sake'. The classical theatre has always been regarded not merely as a place of entertainment, but a place of instruction. It is expected to inculcate and encourage virtuous sentiments. Its plays laud historic acts of courage, filial piety, patriotism and loyalty. Traitors, evil-doers, faithless wives and bad officials invariably suffer a just fate. Thus, after a mythological play in which the chief attraction is the brilliance of the costumes and the dancing, and a rousing martial play in which magnificently garbed warriors strut across the stage on high boots, flags at their backs and duel and cavort and rant grandly in deep guttural tones and fight in battle scenes that are the occasion for expert jugglery and acrobatics—we see the piece of the evening.

The performances have been continuous since six o'clock. It is now nearly ten. The stage is more jewel-like than ever. It gleams with colour out of the semi-darkness of the auditorium. We will see *Killing the Tiger General*, a drama from the Ching dynasty, written about 1644.

The last of the Ming Emperors has been killed. One of his maids enters and in a recitative describes what has happened and expresses her determination to avenge his death. She will impersonate the Princess and thus approach and kill the rebel leader. The actor sings in a high falsetto voice. Most of the audience cannot make out his words (any more than we in the West can make out the words of the usual operatic aria), but they know exactly what he should be saying. They appreciate his grace, his perfect stylised mimicry of feminine charm and determination, his beautiful costume, his strict adherence to the conventions of the classical stage, his masterly control of the long silken 'rippling water sleeves' that flutter over his hands. In between songs he sometimes calls for refreshment—the falsetto makes great demands on the voice. He delicately covers his face with the silken sleeve, and drinks warm tea from a cup. The attendant sometimes walks clear across the stage to serve him, carrying the teapot in its cozy.

In *Scene Two*, indicated merely by a rearrangement of the two chairs on the stage with fresh embroidered cushions and backs—the rebel general enters. He rewards his favourite, the Tiger General with the hand of the supposed Princess. The General is garbed in 'armour' of richly embroidered satin. Four flags project from his shoulder-blades like wings. His boots have soles three inches thick. They add to his height and dignity. His face is painted thickly in black, white and red so that no human feature remains. He never makes one single 'natural' movement. Yet his every gesture and step is instinct with martial strength, ferocity and majesty. In *Scene Three* the Maid is in her finest clothes and prepares to receive the Tiger General. Two attendants bring in a curtain suspended on a bamboo framework. This is a 'bed'. We know therefore that the scene is a 'bedroom'. The Maid infatuates the General, gets him drunk, disarms him and he retires to sleep behind the curtain. The Maid blows out the candles (this indicates that the brilliantly lighted stage is now 'dark') and in the blackness stabs the Tiger General to death. The climax is a moral one, for in the epilogue, her servants upbraid her for committing a murder, though the playwright implies that this is also an act of patriotism —and the Maid then vindicates justice by committing suicide.

After the performance we go 'behind the curtain'. The actors' Greenroom is directly back of the stage. It is filled with 'props'— flags, costumes, boxes. Make-up tables are littered with grease-paints and brushes.

Actors all belong to the Guild and are as a rule even today extremely jealous of their customs and traditions. They have a special temple outside the Hata Gate in Peiping, the shrine of their three patron gods. One is Kuan Yu, the God of War, a hero canonised in the twelfth century; the second is the great Tang Emperor, Ming Huang, founder of the theatrical school of the Pear Garden and legendary creator of the theatrical art as we know it. Ming Huang is said to have himself played the clown and for this reason a clown enjoys special privileges. He is the first to be made up and alone is entitled to sit on any actors' box in the Greenroom. The superstition is that bad luck invariably follows if the actor playing a light female role sits on any box but his own. The third deity is Lin Ming-ju, a little boy who was a pupil of the Pear Garden. All who were friendly to him made rapid progress in their art. His godhead was displayed when he miraculously disappeared. It is the clown too who lights the incense which burns in every Greenroom before the icon of the patron god to whom obeisance is made both before and after every performance.

Origins of the Classical Theatre

Peiping (or as it was formerly called—Peking) is still the acknowledged classical centre of China. It is the birthplace and unofficial headquarters of China's greatest actor—Mei Lan-fang. At its most famous period in modern times, in the 1920's, it had as many as twenty-two theatres, nine restaurants and temples giving regular performances and often a half dozen visiting touring companies for its 800,000 inhabitants. In addition, actors are almost always engaged on the occasion of big banquets, private festivals, weddings or funerals. Most of the regular theatres hold to the classical plan of building such as I have described in Ninghsia. But the biggest is now in Western architectural style— and how inappropriate it seems for Chinese drama! The old imperial playhouses are no longer used. They are museum pieces.

Shanghai, Tientsin, Canton—all the big cities, have their own theatre troupes and are visited regularly by the famous actors. But I have indeed yet to see any Chinese city, town or fair-sized village without its theatre structure. Far in the interior I have come across stages at cross roads or fair grounds. This ubiquity of theatre buildings is a sign of the close relationship that has always existed between the theatre and popular life.

The origins of the classical theatre are closely associated with religious rites. It is known that in 2000 B.C. certain men or women (corresponding to witch-doctors, shamans or priests) performed dances and songs in worship of the gods, to exorcise evil spirits or to supplicate favours from benign influences. Some were probably little more than 'shakers', others gave aesthetic performances highly edifying to their congregations. As these became more closely integrated with imperial ritual they became more elaborately garbed and conventionalised in artistic form.

Temple festivals today have many aspects of a fair and there is usually a secular theatrical troupe performing nearby or jugglers, acrobats, story-tellers and other 'buskers'. There are usually priestly performances of mythological or religious morality plays. But classical drama evidently has been compounded from more than one source. Ancestor worship and the dramatic presentation of the great dead's deeds is such another source. Some authorities suggest that the military plays largely featuring acrobatics and the dexterous wielding of weapons are a survival or development of ancient military ceremonial. Another source undoubtedly are the clowns and jesters employed since ancient times to amuse the court and aristocracy with their witty discourses and antics, or the folk story-tellers and troubadours. The Yangko folk dance drama that has inspired the modern Yangko theatre has also been a source of the classical drama. Yangko is a seasonal festival dance. Even today on the professional stage there are certain seasonal plays (something like our British pantomimes) such as *Crossing the Milky Way*, played on the seventh day of the seventh month or *Chang O's Flight to the Moon*, played at the mid-autumn festival.

There is proof that purely secular performances of a dramatic nature were developed out of religious rites at a comparatively early date—many centuries before our era.

The dance is one of the sources of the Chinese drama. The earliest dances were community affairs performed before the altars as a part of the religious rites. Later, as the dances became more complex, special performers were picked for the leading roles. Still later 'professional' dancers appeared and the dances and dance drama were performed outside their religious context for entertainment. We have descriptions of dance drama from Chow times (1122–314 B.C.). The first Emperor Hsin Shih Huang-ti (255–206 B.C.) had many jesters at his court. Fan-dancers are mentioned with reprobation in the Han dynasty (206 B.C.), as well as masques with actors dressed as gods and animals. Theatrical performances indeed early became an inseparable part of all public festivals and even of the private celebrations of the rich.

Fantastic mythological plays were much in vogue in Han times. The T'ang dynasty (A.D. 618–907) saw a great development of all the arts including the theatre. The great T'ang conquests enriched Chinese civilisation by direct contact with foreign cultures of a high development. The drama became more sophisticated. Satir-ical dialogue was introduced. It is undoubtedly the astonishingly rapid development of the drama at this time that gave rise to the legend that it was the Emperor Ming Huang of the T'ang who founded the Pear Garden college of actors after a visit to the moon where he saw a troupe of performers in the Lunar Monarch's Jade Palace. Even today, actors in China are referred to elegantly as 'Students of the Pear Garden'. Plays of the time however were far from being purely legendary. All the main types already existed: the military heroic play, the mythological, the didactic civilian drama. The comedies and satires did not hesitate to deal with actual social abuses. One T'ang comedy deals with a Mandarin who embezzled public funds. Because of his learning, however, his jail sentence is commuted by the Emperor but he is forced to wear a white robe while for a year the court jesters are allowed to make a mock of him. Back-chat between a 'rotten official' and a foil is a regular curtain raiser in theatres today.

The names of nearly 300 plays of the Sung dynasty (A.D. 960–1278) are known to us. 815 titles have come down from the Yuan dynasty times. This was another fruitful time for the drama. The Yuan dynasty was established by the Mongol conquerors, direct descendants of the Great Khan Ghenghis. In their early years they relied on direct military dictatorship and therefore the Chinese *literati*—the Mandarin bureaucrats, were deprived of their government jobs. There was only one other temporary outlet for their talents—the composition of popular plays and novels, genres that they had previously despised as of no account, but to which they brought sophistication and scholarship. When they regained their power after some 80 years—the Mongol nomads found they could not govern the mighty Chinese empire without their aid—they brought back their interest in the drama to the Courts. Yuan drama is now the classical type of theatre in China. Its extant masterpieces can be seen on every stage.

The theatre continued to flourish under the succeeding dynasty of the Mings, a native dynasty which expelled the alien Mongol conquerors. 600 Ming plays are known, many written by famous scholars, who raised the literary qualities of the drama to greater heights than ever before. Instead of the compact three to five act plays of Yuan times in which one character predominated over all the rest, the Ming dramatists produced play-novels of two to four dozen acts. It is the existence of such plays that has caused the common European belief that Chinese plays continue for several days. In actual fact these plays are seldom if ever shown as one unit. Actors choose only a few scenes from them for a single programme. One of the most famous of these is the *Story of the Lute*, in which a young man is betrothed to a faithful maid, goes to the capital and takes his exams. He becomes a rich Mandarin and is married to an aristocrat by order of the Emperor and is thus prevented from returning home. Meanwhile his parents and girl bride are in the direst straits. Finally his faithful young first wife comes to the capital carrying his lute, makes herself known to him and the drama ends happily.

In these Ming plays development of dramatic action is stressed. Hence the greater number of characters and their greater popularity among the masses of the people. The highly refined and scholastic texts of the Yuan drama in their second period and the complexity of the musical accompaniment to their long dramatic narrations or monologues made them unpopular among the people, but delighted the élite. I shall return to these points again at a later stage.

In 1644 China was conquered again. This time the Manchu dynasty (the Ching), a barbarian house from Manchuria, ascended the Dragon throne. But the Manchus, like the Yuans, quickly absorbed Chinese culture. The reigns of Kang Hsi (1662—1723) and Chien Lung (1736–95) were notable for a great renaissance of the arts, caused in part by the extended intercourse of China with foreign cultural trends under an expanding military and commercial policy. The theatre too flourished and over 800 plays of some merit have come down to us from that period. Historical tragedy was greatly in vogue. *The Blood-Stained Fan* dealing with the last days of the Mings and the *Palace of Eternal Life* dealing with the T'ang Emperor Ming Huang and his notorious concubine Yang Kuei-fei—a sort of Chinese Dubarry—are perenially popular even today. The chief innovation however of the time is the dramatisation of the famous novels such as the *Three Kingdoms* (dealing with the feudal wars and heroes of (265–221 B.C.) much in the vein of the English *Knights of the Round Table*) written in the Yuan dynasty, or the *Heroes of the Water Hole*, a Chinese Robin Hood tale, or the ever famous love story *The Dream of the Red Chamber*. Dramatisations from this great novel are of very recent date. China's finest actor today—Mei Lan-fang—is their introducer. He spans two epochs. The Manchu dynasty ended in 1911. In that year the Chinese Republic was founded.

It is interesting to note that it was only in the Manchu dynasty that women were forbidden to appear on the stage. This was because in the corrupt later days of the preceding Ming dynasty, Princes and officials kept large numbers of actresses in their palaces and this led to gross immorality and abuses. The Manchu barbarian conquerors, wishing to preserve their manhood from similar corruption, banned women from the stage.

The virile Manchus however also fell under the spell of the theatre and towards the end of the dynasty large numbers of the idle aristocracy took up amateur theatricals. Many fine stages can still be seen in the Manchu palaces in Peiping. Usually they are of the form I have already described, though more lavish in decoration. Some however have two stages, one above the other. The lower is used for 'mortal' actors, the upper for 'Celestial' beings. One theatre even has three stages, the lowest one of all being used for the actions of denizens of the nether regions.

Whereas in very early days, stages in public places were temporary affairs built of bamboo and matting, later more permanent stages were built, both in temples and public community centres. Still later they were built in tea-houses, for the entertainment of the patrons. At first the charges were made only for the tea, but later when the play became the thing, the theatre was still called a 'tea-house' and the audience continued to sit at tables and sip tea. This close retention of tradition is as we have already seen a feature of the theatre. The two pillars supporting the stage canopy are always red or black lacquered. Actors always enter by the left door and exit through the right. The place where the orchestra sits is still called the 'Nine Dragon Entrance' (*Chiu Lung Kou*). This name, writes Miss Zung in her informative book, originates from a practice of the Emperor Ming Huang of the T'ang dynasty.

He was so fond of music that when his favourite, the beautiful Yang Kuei-fei danced, he himself directed the orchestra. Nine dragons—symbols of the Emperor—were carved on the platform where he sat. Every actor as he appeared had to pass His Majesty and pay him respect before he took the centre of the stage, and receive a momentary glance of appraisal by the fastidious monarch. Now, even though the orchestra does not always sit at this spot the name still attaches to it and every actor on entering, pauses here to perform some gesture or movement to permit the audience to inspect and classify him.

Characters, Make-up, Costumes, Props, Scenery, Music, Gestures, The Plays

The admirer of the classical theatre in China approaches the object of his entertainment in much the same way as the balleto-mane in the West approaches the classical ballet. He knows the story of the play from A to Z. He knows exactly the traditional gesture that the heroine, for instance, will make in the *Rainbow Pass* when the Widow, filled with thoughts of revenge, meets the slayer of her husband—and falls in love with him, but he will be enchanted by the special nuances, the skill with which the actor performs that significant gesture—the climax of the play in which hate turns to love. The Chinese theatre-goer knows the popular songs and music; he knows how the costumes should look, but he enjoys what one may call 'legitimate' departures from the tradi-tion. Yet naturally only the élite, the real dilettantes, know all the many extant plays. If, for instance, during the performance of one of the difficult Yuan pieces you ask an average member of the audience what exactly the actor said, the answer is usually only a rough paraphrase. The songs in fact are often almost unintelligible except to the initiated. Thus it is a great aid to have a knowledge —which is possessed by almost every theatre-goer—of the in-numerable keys to understanding of the play—a knowledge of

22

the conventions of the classical Chinese drama, symbols of colour, costume, gesture, intonation, music, make-up and scenery.

The predominance of yellow indicates a member of the Imperial House; light yellow itself is the colour of the Emperor. Honourable people wear red; the virtuous and kind wear blue. The brusque and straightforward are symbolised by black. But the symbolism of colours is modified by other considerations. White, for instance, is the colour of the very young, but a man with a white butterfly-shaped smudge on his face is a clown.

The costumes are mainly based on ancient models, though robes of the Manchu times are sometimes worn. Mei Lan-fang's wardrobe follows the fashions of the T'ang dynasty of more than one thousand years ago.

As a general rule, however, there is no attempt at historical accuracy in costumes so long as they be beautiful. A first-rate company prides itself on the uniform magnificence and good taste of its costumes and sets of accessory embroideries for tables, chairs, canopies and flags—the only 'scenery' employed. A beggar will be garbed in clothes symbolising poverty and rags—his garments

Comic Mandarin of the
Classical Theatre

are covered with irregular patches of colour—but they will all be exquisitely blended and made of rich silks or satin. Characters in a typical classical drama are really 'types', thus their costumes are not 'individualised' but 'typified'. An 'official' character, a magistrate, a mandarin or an Imperial Minister, wears an orthodox official robe known as a *mang*, made of stiff satin. This has a round collar and long silken sleeves, slit and falling from the wrist—the 'rippling water sleeves'—it is embroidered with dragon designs and the stylised 'water-wave' pattern around the lower edge. He wears a precious stone belt, *yu tai*, around his waist. This is of some stiff material studded with glass mirrors and imitation precious stones and it encircles the waist like a large hoop, fixed at the back and hanging in front. On ordinary occasions the official wears the *Tieh Tzu*, a simpler coatee of satin, sometimes in plain black or other colour or embroidered also with 'rippling water sleeves'. It is belted with a sash. Good officials wear square hats; scoundrels wear round ones.

The *Chun* is a skirt worn only by female characters. It may be plain or richly embroidered. When fastened high above the chest it indicates a poor, distressed woman. On occasions—depending on the context of the action—it symbolises a traveller on a long journey, for it shows that the character is not properly clad. It would for instance be fitting for the heroine in the *Song of the Lute* to wear the *Chun* in this way when, after her long journey, she enters the capital in search of her husband.

The *K'u Ao* is a blouse and trousers; the *Chun Ao* is a blouse and skirt, usually richly embroidered with silk thread or sequins, worn by a coquettish young woman. The young sing-song girl in the play I have described wore a richly embroidered white and pink *K'u Ao* when she was brought before the magistrate.

The cape is worn to show that the character is travelling or has just been aroused from bed, as in illness, or being outdoors late at night.

Military characters on state occasions or on the battlefield wear the resplendent armour, *Kai Kao*. This is the most spectacular costume in the actor's wardrobe. It is made of patterned satin, richly and heavily embroidered with gold and silver, and in the brightest colours. Four separate panels of material hang from the waist. The central front panel is embroidered with a fearsome dragon or tiger head at the waist. A 'heart-protecting mirror' covers the breast. The *Kai Kao* of an amazon has many vari-coloured streamers hanging from the waist, often tipped with tiny bells. Generals wear four flags embroidered in their colours rising like wings from their backs. These are derived from the fact that in ancient days generals in the field gave pennants to their personal messengers as proof of the authenticity of orders.

At first only robber chiefs or rebel generals on the stage wore the gorgeous pheasant tails from seven to eight feet in length as decorations from their helms, but now generals of all kinds, but especially female or young com-manders, sport these supple, graceful plumes. The general movements of playing with the feathers is the same, but *Ch'in* (painted face char-acters—Generals, Em-perors, Princes) when

A General of the Classical Theatre

they hold them by the tips of their fingers, balance them higher than *Lao Shen* (aged male characters), while the *Tan* (female character) holds them gracefully only a little above shoulder level. Each set figure in feather dancing has its own symbolic meaning. For instance, anger or determination is shown by 'winding the feathers'—dropping the head forward and then tossing it in a circular movement so that the feathers move and bend in a perfect circle. Surprise, contemplation or re-collection are shown by 'nodding the feathers' so that the tips touch the floor just in front of the actor as the head is lowered, and then thrown back as the head is raised. Both tips must, however, move in absolute and unruffled rhythm and unison. The utmost firm determination is demonstrated in a most effective way by holding the feathers' tips between the teeth.

In 'dancing with the feathers', they are held about a foot from the tip, starting with both hands in front of the chest. The left hand is then moved inward and the right outward in consecutive circles. It is not permissible to move both hands inward or outward at the same time. In these and other movements the audience is delighted by the perfect rhythm and symmetry of design with which the feathers are handled and manipulated.

A nun or a monk habitually wears a cape or grey or yellow coat, but occasionally a different style of clothing is permitted for added dramatic effect. Mei Lan-fang, whose great prestige as an artist of the highest artistic integrity permits him to do many things that would be considered impermissibly bumptious in one of lesser fame, in his dance drama of *A Nun in Search of Love*, wears a *Tieh Tƺe* under a long sleeveless jacket embroidered with dark-coloured, diamond-shaped appliqués, the whole in rich, soft silk. In representing a beggar the actor's *Tieh Tƺe* is artistically patched with irregularly shaped pieces of silk. It is characteristic of the philosophy of the Chinese classical drama that this costume is colloquially known in dramatic literature as 'the dress of the rich and noble'—meaning that its wearer may sometime gain wealth and a higher social standing, because modesty and humility will always triumph over evil or adversity.

Stage Properties

There is no 'picture-frame stage', no 'box of illusions' in the classical Chinese theatre. There is no stage scenery therefore aiming to create the illusionary effect of reality on the stage. The stage is open to view from three sides and spectators not infrequently, as in the Elizabethan theatre, take their seats right on the edges of the stage itself.

As in some modern productions of the West (derived in fact partly from the study of the Chinese classical stage) or the *Commedia del'Arte*, the Chinese classical theatre creates a theatrical world of its own and gives merely certain necessary hints as to the place and time of the action, which the imagination of the spectator is free to expand as he lists. Thus, while there is no scenery in the usual Western sense, there are numerous stage properties which are mainly in fact 'props' for the audiences' imagination. Many of the actors' conventionalised gestures are similarly 'props'.

In the play *The Strategy of the Unguarded City*, the crafty general Chu Ko-liang (of the *Three Kingdoms* novel) fools the attacking enemy. When his opponents approach, they find the city gates wide open and two unarmed soldiers sweeping the road before it. Up on the battlements sits Chu Ko-liang playing tranquilly on the *ch'in*. Suspecting a trap, though in fact the city has no garrison, the enemy withdraws. This short play about an immensely popular historical character, the theme of calm in the face of stress which has a special attraction for Chinese imaginations nurtured on an admiration for *Tao*, the Way, invariably stills the most gossipy audience. There is in addition fine singing and gorgeous military costumes. Yet it seems incongruous to no one but the uninitiated, that General Chu enters and in full view of the audience, takes his seat on a chair atop a table which has just been placed there by a stage attendant. In front of him two other attendants hold up a bamboo frame which supports a screen painted with a city gate in a brick wall about five feet high. When the scene ends the attendants remove the 'wall', roll it up and take it away. The table is brought back to the centre of the stage, the chairs rearranged on either side of it, they are covered with fresh embroideries—and the stage is now a 'council chamber'.

A conventionalised 'mountain and stream' design painted on a similar screen and propped up by a table or chair represents or indicates that the action is taking place in the highlands. A character in a 'chariot' enters the stage preceded by two attendants each holding horizontally a square flag on which a wheel with spokes is drawn.

Banners decorated with a 'waves and fishes' design are brought on the stage by attendants to indicate water, the sea or a great river. A character committing suicide by drowning jumps towards them. The attendants fold the flags around him and all exit together at a swift pace. At the end of a 'battle', the defeated or killed protagonist does not need to fall. He exits at a run. The victor makes a flourish of arms and then exits with dignity to the clash of cymbals and clappers.

A table and two chairs are about the only two 'constructions' which a classical theatre needs for its stage. A chair can serve as a 'prison'. The imprisoned actor stands behind it and looks through barred windows by peering through the back supports. A chair can be a 'well'. If an actor, depending on the play's context, jumps upon it and then down on the other side and then makes a hurried exit—all this is prefaced with the gestures indicating a fatal decision—then he has jumped down a well and drowned himself.

Men in a besieged city run in circles across the stage against the background of the city wall but in opposite directions to each other. Armies are indicated by attendants, carrying banners, each signifying one or two thousand men. Black banners indicate a storm. Actors or attendants in fours run across the stage with these to show the storm's approach. If an attendant approaches the actors and throws white bits of paper over them like confetti at a wedding you will know that it is snowing hard.

A whip about three feet long and with four tassels of silk evenly spaced along its length indicates a horse. An actor entering with such a whip in his right hand is immediately understood to be riding. Raising and bending his leg in a conventional gesture he shows that he is dismounting or mounting. He throws his whip to the floor—that is, he has let his horse loose to graze. The carrying of a lantern or a candle indicates that it is evening or dark. An oar indicates a ship or a boat. A yellow scroll with the ideographs for 'Royal Mandate', carried so that they face the audience, indicates an imperial proclamation or message. This is frequently the *deus ex machina* of a classical play. It solves many a third act tangle, brings confusion to the villain and wealth, wife and happiness to the hero. A huge wooden block wrapped in yellow silk represents the imperial seal. A bed or bedroom is indicated by an embroidered curtain on a bamboo frame somewhat like the side view of a four-poster bed. When a character is beheaded, he falls to the ground for a moment, then rises and quickly runs off-stage. An attendant then produces a bundle shaped like a head and wrapped in red cloth which is then displayed to the audience. In Ninghsia I saw a play about a devil. Whenever the devil manifested his power, an attendant standing on the side of the stage would let off fire-crackers. When the devil cast flames at another character, the attendant walked up to him with the nonchalance of some invisible man and, striking a match, set fire to a spirit-soaked bunch of tissue paper and whisked this around him.

The Music

'Raucous', 'ear-splitting', 'noise'—these are some of the usual descriptions which Europeans give to their first acquaintance with Chinese stage music. Certainly the constant use of the horns, the time-beater made of wood, the drums, gongs, cymbals and bells is difficult to get accustomed to. Even the Chinese violin, the *Hu Ch'in* is a difficult instrument to get used to. It is made of a hollowed bamboo stem about seven inches long, covered with snake skin to make a sound box. It has a high-pitched, wailing note, its passages seem to run on interminably and its range is small. This

Horse whip   Spirit whisk
Oar   Lantern
Chariot Flag   Water Flag

City Wall

Props in the Classical Chinese theatre

is the usual accompaniment to song or recitative. Only the *Pi Pa*, the lute, or the *Yueh Ch'in*, the Moon guitar, or the flutes of *Sheng*,

the small reed organ, have a timbre, or melody-making qualities which are familiar to the ear trained on Western music.

Music is an integral part of the performance. Indeed, plays are distinguished by the type of music they employ.[1] Music accompanies the songs and dances. It intensifies and forms a framework of sound for action and gesture. Some passages however are decorative bridges, *Ku Men* ('through the door' literally) which give the actor time to rest his voice or prepare himself, because the falsetto style of singing makes great demands on an actor's powers of voice.

Character Types and Make-up

The classical drama has a certain number of set character types. This is analogous to the Western classical ballet, which has such set types as the Prince, the Princess, the King and Queen who are expected to, and do, invariably dance and act in certain set ways.

Tan with spears

In the Chinese theatre, the four most important types are: the *Sheng* (males), the *Tan* (females), the *Chou* (clowns), and the *Chin* (the 'painted-face characters').

The *Cheng Sheng* is an elderly man with a long beard, usually an Emperor, a General or a faithful servant. A related character type is the *Hsiao Sheng*, a youthful civilian or military character. This is frequently a young scholar and lover, who carries a fan, or a military man, who wears the proud pheasant feathers.

The *Hua Tan* is a coquettish, worldly wise young woman. A variation of this type is the *Wu Tan* or warrior maid. Mei Lan-fang,

---

[1] See section on types of plays, page 41.

'Trisected' face—a
General

White-powdered face—
a Scoundrel

Make-up for God of
Fire

A wicked, stupid Mandarin
with beard.

who was trained to act these latter female types, has made them pre-eminent on the classical stage today just as, in the last generation, the famous actor T'an Shen-pei of Peking, who died in 1919, made the type of the *Cheng Sheng*, the upright old man, the central figure of a whole theatrical period. The *Ching I* is a female character, an honest, simple type. She is often the victim of adverse circumstance but is always a model of fortitude. Such for instance is the young wife in the *Song of the Lute*.

These two types of characters, the *Sheng* and *Tan*, wear heavy make-up according to Western theatrical standards, but their faces still retain their natural lines. Make-up merely accentuates certain features, as for instance the alabaster whiteness of a beautiful young girl, or the wrinkles and grey, sparse hair on an old man's face. For a *Tan*, Chinese ink is dropped into the pupil of the eye to make it large and brilliant. The young hero's eyes and brows are drawn up by means of adhesive tape to give them a noble slant. Artificial braids are added to the *Tan's* head-dress. An old man wears an artificial beard. In the old days this used to be affixed direct on to the face by means of wires and paint; now, in order to free the actor's mouth and chin for declamation, it is affixed by means of wires slightly in front of the mouth and face. Though the actor in his development of these characters moves within certain more or less fixed bounds, and his gestures—such as mounting a horse, opening or closing a door, or entering a boat —follow the fixed patterns of classical movement—he still has a fairly wide field of actions in which he can improvise according to his own aesthetic sense. It is for this reason that the outstanding actors like Mei Lan-fang or T'an Shen-pei have been exponents of such roles. In addition to the artistry which they display in performing the set patterns of movement (analogous to the five fundamental movements of the Western classical ballet), they have introduced certain extra outstanding traits of individuality of

C

interpretation in their roles that make all the difference between a 'good' actor and a genius.

Two other female character types must be mentioned: the *Lao Tan*, a dignified old woman or mother and the *Chou Tan*—the comedienne. Actors who specialise in the role of serious *tan* characters appear to imitate with astonishing verisimilitude the somewhat simpering, almost tottering gait of a woman with tiny bound feet or 'lily feet', as they are euphemistically called. In actual fact they wear special small wooden 'feet' made in the form of shoes and walk on tiptoe very much like a ballet dancer or a woman in very high-heeled wedge shoes. While giving the exact effect of the bound feet, however, these considerably increase the difficulties of the actor, especially in dance and acrobatic sequences.

The third main character is the *Chou*, the clown or comedian. This character has the greatest latitude of action of all. His costume is often fantastic and he takes pleasure in breaking the conventions of the stage. His make-up—like that of clowns in the Western circus or pantomime—is not realistic but conventional, a smudge of white on his face, bright red cheeks, sometimes just a highly powdered white nose if he is a military type of comedian. He may sing or dance in a burlesque way. He may use the everyday form of speech; he may entirely break through the conventional barrier between the stage and the audience to address it directly. His allusions even in a supposedly historic scene can be completely local and typical. He can range from sophisticated wit to knockabout.

The fourth main type of the classical stage is the *Chin*—the 'painted-face character', in which the make-up is so thickly applied that it forms a mask (such as, for example, Pantaloon wears in a Christmas pantomime), sometimes so arbitrary in design that the natural lines of the face are completely obscured. The major character of this type is the *Wu Sheng*, the warrior, skilled in stage fighting and acrobatics. Every evening's entertainment includes a play chosen to star the best *Wu Sheng* actor. The military costume is the most effective and rich on the stage. The actor's face is heavily made up in bright colours and crowned with a magnificent head-dress. His costume is studded with mirrors and gems. Every gesture is conventional and replete with dignity and awesome majesty. The extra height given by the thick soled boots, the flags and weapons make him a fitting image of the panoply of war and power. In the fighting climax in which rhythm and acrobatics, skill and grace are combined, the orchestra accentuates the excitement with the crash of cymbals and gongs.

Other characters in the *Chin* type are the good 'black-faced' types or the evil 'white powdered face' types, and various *Ta Chin* types whose character for good or evil is indicated by the colours and design of his face make-up. Such a 'painted-face' character may be a wicked or a good minister, a rebel general or a bandit. Finally there are various mythological types, gods, demons, or animals in semi-human form, with their symbolic designs of face make-up.

Up to the time of the Ming dynasty (A.D. 1368) only the wicked characters wore heavy, 'unnatural' make-up. Their degree of wickedness or craftiness was, and is today, in direct proportion to the area of white on their faces. In the preceding Yuan dynasty, as we have already indicated, the range of characters in the early classical theatre was limited and only the *Sheng* and *Tan* characters played leading roles, hence there was little emphasis on the parts that later became 'painted-face' types and hence little attempt to develop their costume or make-up. Under the Mings, the long narrative 'novel' plays with their many characters demanded some method of identifying the minor characters, hence the development of make-up conventions, which strictly defined which characters should wear which type of make-up. The practice of warriors in earlier times painting their faces in order to strike awe into their enemies undoubtedly influenced the actual designs used for the characters.

Following the Ming period, make-up designs became more and more complex, with an elaborate symbolism of colour and form. Red symbolises loyalty and uprightness, Purple shows these traits in a lesser degree and also indicates old age. Black shows simplicity and straightforwardness; Blue, obstinacy and ferocity. Yellow denotes craftiness or cleverness. Gold and Silver are the colours of dignity and are used on the faces of gods and fairies. Green is the colour of wicked ghosts and devils. Pink and Grey are the colours of old age. White painted over the entire face, covering the upper part of the face and nose, the centre of the face, and the nose only, indicates the four degrees of wickedness. Certain special symbols are used to indicate specific characters such as the cloud design for the God of the Clouds, the fire design for the Fire God. A moon shape on the forehead indicates the famous judge Pao Tsen who could journey to the other world to interrogate the spirits of the dead.

The make-up of well-known characters has often remained stable over considerable periods of time. Others have been gradually modified by famous actors whose prestige is sufficient to establish and set a new standard. By means of their make-up, actors can also signify their own individual attitude of respect or contempt for the historical characters they portray.

Gestures

Just as each character type has its own special costume, its own special type of make-up, its typical 'property' attributes and often its own special musical introductory passages, so does it have a codified set of intonations, gestures and whole patterns of dance or pantomime movements, some of which are special to a particular type, some of which are used interchangeably by different types. Laughter for instance is divided into about twenty typical kinds beginning with 'happy laughter', 'cold laughter', 'conceited laughter', and ending with 'flattering laughter', 'uneasy laughter' or 'insane laughter'. To laugh violently the actor laughs three times with upheld hands. 'Flattering laughter' is special to a 'white-faced' character.

There has not yet been sufficient scientific research on the Chinese theatre to determine the exact why and wherefore of all its conventions. In some cases origins can be directly traced, while some are of comparatively recent date. In most cases only hints can be given of their origins. It is known for instance that many centuries ago the actor's sleeves extended for a foot or more beyond the hand. This would not be unusual. Many Eastern peoples, including the Mongols who conquered China (the Yuan dynasty) still wear such long sleeves as the style of their everyday dress, but it is not known for certain when the actors substituted for the long thick sleeve the artificial long cuff of light white silk about a foot or two long attached to the ordinary sleeve and left open at the seam. This is the 'rippling water sleeve' which is invariably associated with certain costumes and types. It seems safe to conjecture however, that the long silken sleeve also derives in part from the dance. In ancient days the movements of the hand and sleeve were of major importance in the dance, and the dance played an even greater role in dramatic representations than it does today. Comparisons between the names of movements and gestures used today in the theatre and those mentioned in ancient manuscripts and memorials, show that the basic form of dance drama as we know it today was established as early as the T'ang dynasty (A.D. 618–907). This dance drama included some of the basic movements which have now been incorporated as an integral part of the pantomime and gestures of the ordinary drama, in which dancing as such does not take place. Thus it is that the student actor is trained not only in voice production and acting, but in acrobatics and dancing, with special reference to the hand, the fingers, the arm, the foot, leg and waist.

The *Tan* actor trains in at least fifty different kinds of 'sleeve movement', each with its own particular pattern of grace and symmetry and symbolic or directly expressive connotation.

As the actor enters on to the stage he pauses at the 'Nine Dragon Place', he moves his right and then his left hand, palm inwards, from just below his chest, downwards in a half circle. At the base of the turn, just above the slightly bent knee, with a quick fling and turn of the wrist, he flicks the silken sleeve backwards. This, 'the turning sleeve' movement, is a signal for the orchestra to be ready. But it is also a demonstration before the audience. In its execution alone the audience is able to judge of the actor's grace, his timing, his control, his mastery of the theatrical art.

The sleeve is used to show embarrassment by being held before the face. This also indicates that the actor is hidden from the other personages on the stage. The 'running sleeve' as performed by such an artist as Mei Lan-fang, is instinct with the grace and charm, the fluttering tremulousness of a young maid. The sleeve is thrown upward, allowed to hang free from the wrist, trailing as he runs in a slanting curve with the right hand held slightly higher than the head. In this movement it is aesthetically impermissible for the actor to run straight forwards.

As he approaches the centre of the stage after his entrance, the actor faces slightly to the right, raises his left hand to the level of his chin, while, with his bare right hand, he holds the lower corner of the left sleeve. In this position, 'the introduction sleeve', he sings the prologue of the next action. It indicates that he is 'still' an actor. As he finally announces the name of the character he is to play, he lowers his arms slightly and thus shows that he is 'in character'.

The 'weeping' actor holds the upper corner of the left sleeve with the right hand and raises it to his eyes, inclining the head as if in tears. These are but a few of the 'sleeve movements'.

No less strict is the training for control of the hands in a whole vocabulary of symbolism. For instance, the only time that a maid is allowed to extend two fingers of a hand is when, in fencing, the hand is brought forward, first and second fingers extended, thumb and third finger touching their tips, gently rounded, while the small finger is curved naturally.

Even such actions as pointing forward or back, raising the hand to the head in thought, supplicating, repulsing, greeting—these are all as rigidly patterned as the steps of a classical ballerina. The same is true of body and feet movements, and such actions as sitting, slipping, running. When an actor represents a ghost he walks stiff and erect with small steps and with arms hanging at his sides. If a ghost takes a long journey he whirls around three times— symbolic of the whirlwind on which Chinese ghosts are habitually reputed to ride

Convention governs the more complicated movements as well. An actor never takes up a real brush to write with. He picks up an imaginary one in his right hand, then with the thumb and middle finger of the left hand he removes any loosened hairs from its tip and flicks them away. To show that he is crossing a threshold, the actor lifts his right foot as if he were stepping over the door-sill (which in old Chinese houses is often ten inches high). In opening or closing doors, the movements of holding the lock, inserting the key, removing the lock or opening the bolts and pushing aside the leaves and so on are done in graceful, stylised and unchanging pantomime. Strict convention also governs the movements of mounting or dismounting from an imaginary horse. When a 'horse' is led on, the actor holds the tasselled whip vertically by the handle with its tip either up or down In every case, music, led by the time-beater, controls the rhythm of the actions.

Taking a seat is never done in a natural or 'naturalistic' way, but according to a set pattern. Standing, for instance, at the centre of the stage with the chair behind him, the actor turns left and walks towards the chair along an S-shaped route, then he turns right about to face the audience again as he approaches the chair, stops when his back is directly in front of it, and only then sits down. If two characters enter to take their seats from opposite sides of the stage, they approach the front centre of the stage and then take interwoven S-shaped paths in reverse order before finally seating themselves. There is an engaging flourish about this circumlocutory way of taking a seat.

Boating scenes provide delightful interludes of choreographic pantomime. This is one of the attractions of such a play as *The Valiant Fisherman and his Daughter* as played by Mei Lan-fang.

When the fisherman, in one scene, enters holding an oar, through the opening usually reserved for exits, this shows that he is already in his boat. He disembarks by placing his oar on the stage and then jumping briskly 'ashore'. Then he draws the imaginary boat towards him with a hand over hand movement as on a rope and makes it fast, pantomiming the motions of tying a knot. To get back into his imaginary boat he jumps forward, flexes his knees and sways as if balancing the craft, then he picks up the oar or is handed it by an attendant and 'rows' off. The *Tan* (young women characters) have particularly happy chances for delightful dance pantomime sequences as in 'rolling up the curtains' or 'weaving' or 'making shoe thread'.

The Actor

In the West it often happens that some talented adult amateur actor decides to take up the stage for a career and makes a big success of it. No such instance has ever been recorded of the professional classical Chinese theatre. This is not only because the actors themselves have hitherto formed a close guild with jealously guarded traditions, and because, with the exception of a few top-ranking stars, rates of remuneration are not by any means generous (in fact there is chronic unemployment among the lower grades and 'supers'), but because the demands made on the

voice of a good actor can only be met by long and exacting training. Intensive training is also needed before an actor gains such
mastery of classical movement and gesture, that, like Mei Lan-
fang, the onlooker becomes unconscious of the technique and is
free to admire only the exquisite art. For this reason, training
begins in early youth and lasts for six to seven years. There is no
special actors' school, no mythical Pear Garden. The would-be
actor studies as an apprentice with some old actor and completes
his training in the boys' troupes.

The social status of the actor has changed considerably for the
better in recent years. Though aristocratic amateurs under the
Manchus delighted to appear with professionals at private performances, as a general rule, the actor was regarded as belonging
to the lowest caste. During the Manchu times, only men acted,
and because of this their morals were suspect and in many
cases rightly notorious. It is only in modern times that special
female troupes have appeared (in which women play men's parts),
and even mixed troupes of men and women. It is the rise of such
outstanding personalities as Mei Lan-fang, Yu Shu-jen or Ch'en
Ten-tsui however, who have raised the status of the actor and
made theirs an honoured profession. Mei Lan-fang has received
official honours under the Republic. His tours to Russia and other
countries have been sponsored by the state. In the old days, the
dilettantes of the stage were to be found chiefly among the Manchu
aristocracy. Today, a surprising number of the middle classes
among the intellectuals in schools and colleges maintain classical
theatre club troupes.

Types of Plays

It was during the Mongol Yuan dynasty (1260–1368) that the
classical theatre came to be divided into the Northern (*Tsa Chü*)
and Southern (*Hsi Wen*) styles, which is still the main division
today. This corresponds to the definition that took place in

classical painting at a somewhat earlier date, as a result of which the Northern School became noted for its strict adherence to classical tradition, while the Southern School—within the general style of the feudal epoch—was more realist and impressionist.

The typical Northern or *Tsa Chü* play is divided into four 'turns' in each of which a *Shen* or *Tan* character plays the leading role. The minor characters usually appear first and start off the action. The leading character then enters, declaims an introductory passage of poetry and a self-introduction which describes his past life history and his present state. ('I am so-and-so, a poor orphan, abandoned by my parents during the disturbances of war. I have now come to the city, etc., etc. . . .') This is followed by the dialogue and drama itself.

The typical Southern, *Hsi Wen*, play initiated in Yuan times and further developed under the Mings, runs to as many as forty-five scenes as, for instance, in the *Tale of the Lute*. Both types use the various conventions of scenery, costume and make-up we have previously described, but in the Southern type there is a relatively freer flow to the action. Singing, dancing, recitative, poetry, declamation or even duets are interwoven with unending invention into its dramatic pattern. In the Northern style, monologues mainly carry the 'action'; in the Southern, dramatic action predominates.

In the Northern, *Tsa Chü*, songs are arranged in sets having the same key. Typical of its stricter conventions is the fact that all lines in any set have the same rhyme, and they are sung in the standard dialect of Kaifeng in Honan Province, ancient capital of the Sung dynasty. Such plays are also permitted to have tragic endings. Those of the Southern *Hsi Wen* style always have happy endings; Good invariably triumphs over Evil, Honesty over Dishonesty and Love over Hate. The heroes are always paragons of filial piety—the outstanding virtue according to Confucianism.

In the North, the lute leads the orchestra. Pauses are emphasised in singing. Clarity of tone and enunciation is paramount, though the archaic, scholastic phraseology is hard to follow except for the intelligentsia. The Southern song is led by the wooden time-beater and the sweet note of the flute. It emphasises emotional expressiveness, is more flexible and sweet to the ear but permits the words to be prolonged until they are almost unintelligible. Dancing is a more frequent element than in the Northern style.

These two basic types of the classical drama today each have subsidiary styles modified as to musical accompaniment by the influence of alien cultures and local provincial innovations. In the early Ching dynasty days the *Pi Huang* style was developed in Anhwei Province (Central China) in which the *Hu Ch'in* violin is the main accompaniment of the songs. This is also a feature of the similar and even more popular *Er Huang* style developed in nearby Hupeh Province, or the boisterous *Pan Tzu* style that comes from the Northern province of Shansi and which is also remarkable for the extensive use of the time-beater, *Pan*.

The *Kun Chu* style originated earlier in Ming times as a vehicle for the popular romantic love stories, which contrast so sharply with the primarily ethical dramas of the Northern styles. It is associated with the town of Soochow in South China. When this place was devastated in the Taiping Peasant Rebellion of 1856, the *Kun Chu* style suffered a loss that even the establishment in 1921 of a *Kun Chu* Renaissance Institute by some rich theatre patrons of Soochow, has been unable to repair. But Mei Lan-fang has revived its finest features in his own troupe. Here the flute is the main instrument.

All of these styles can be seen today on the contemporary classical stage.

The Role of the Classical Drama

No exhaustive scientific or indeed aesthetic analysis has ever been attempted which would explain the full reasons for the conventions of the Chinese classical theatre. However, it is clear that the general underlying *raison d'être* of these conventions will be found in its genesis from religious and imperial ceremonial of remote times and in its maturing through the feudal period of Chinese history, with its characteristic ideology. Analogies immediately spring to mind from European religious and feudal ceremonial, the symbolic tragedy which lies at the heart of the Roman Catholic Mass, the *mysteries* and early Elizabethan *masques* and other symbolic or ritual performances in which real personages and actions are idealised and conventionalised in conformity with the prevailing metaphysical and scholastic philosophy.

The didactic, propagandist and moralistic nature of the theatre becomes quite understandable when viewed in this historic light. The Classical theatre presents certain typical personages, not individualised characters as in the modern Western theatre. They act in certain set ways, with certain set gestures. Their actions lead to results which are ordained of necessity by a certain unchanging code of morality (Confucian morality). The Gods, or the Imperial Mandate constantly appear as the *deus ex machina* that solves all problems. All this becomes understandable in general outline when viewed in the light of the feudal conditions of dynastic China, under which the classical drama developed. Here in actual life— and the theatre mirrors life—we have strictly ordained hierarchic divisions of society, in which all facets of life are prescribed by the Confucian codes and ritual, and there is implicit belief in the actual presence of Gods, the spirits of the ancestors and the Divine Right and power of the Monarch. There is implicit belief that the celestials intervene constantly in mundane affairs. The universal acceptance of the theatre as a place for moral uplift stems from the almost universal Chinese acceptance of Confucian doctrine that stresses the efficacy of music and the arts as a means of civilising the turbulent spirit of man and guiding the barbarian into acceptance of the Chinese way of life.

Within the limits set by that way of life and thought however, the Chinese classical theatre has achieved a high level of artistic development, higher I believe than that achieved by any comparable theatrical form. It is for this reason that it has maintained its astonishing vitality and popularity right up to the present, and that performances by Mei Lan-fang in Russia and Japan or indeed anywhere else have been hailed as artistic events of the first importance.

The vast mass of China's 450,000,000 population are still keen devotees of the classical drama. An increasing number of them however, particularly the revolutionary democrats among all classes, are no longer satisfied with its intellectual fare. They are demanding a modern theatrical art that will have the same significant relationship to modern industrial and democratic society as the classical theatre had to agricultural and feudal society.

During the revolutionary social upheaval in China it is not surprising therefore that the ruling groups around the dictator Chiang Kai-shek tended to patronise the classical theatre at the expense of the various modern theatres. A few of the classical dramas are banned on grounds of morality, but the Yangko theatre of the Communist-led areas of China was completely banned in the Chiang Kai-shek ruled areas, while the modern Western style theatre, popular among the revolutionary students, suffered under crippling police censorship. In some Kuomintang ruled provinces it was censored out of existence.

Outstanding exponents of the classical drama, feeling the need to bring their art into tune with the modern trends of thought in China, are reviving classical plays which have revolutionary implications. Mei Lan-fang has popularised the *Valiant Fisherman and his Daughter* who, oppressed by wicked officials, take summary revenge and then depart to join the 'Green Forest Men' (outlaws). Others of his plays stress the anciently recognised Chinese 'right of revolution' against unjust rulers. His advancement of the

Tan (female role), to pre-eminence is in itself an expression of the new position of women in Chinese life.

It would be a great mistake to believe that the days of the classical drama are over. There will, undoubtedly, be modifications of its form and content, but as actual practice in the new urban centres and revolutionary areas of North and Central China, have shown, the roots of this art are sunk deep in the soul of the people and are still drawing fresh vitality therefrom.

CHAPTER TWO

THE
WESTERN
STYLE

IN 1915 A group of Chinese students who had studied in Japan —then the nearest centre of 'Western culture'—and there become acquainted with modern Western theatrical art, returned to China and founded the *Spring Willow Dramatic Society* in Peking, or as it is now known, Peiping. They were determined to reform the Chinese theatre. They loudly decried the classical drama which was the only style of theatre that China at that time knew. They denounced it as old-fashioned, as feudal. Many of them claimed that it should be scrapped altogether because it was a brake on China's progress. The *Spring Willow* society aimed to create a modern Western style theatre for China that would present both foreign and Chinese plays with a modern outlook. *La Dame aux Camelias* and *Uncle Tom's Cabin* were two of their first efforts.

As was to be expected, the 'Western style' drama found little favour with the popular masses and was disdained by the old Mandarin intellectuals as 'un-Chinese'—a sufficient reason for complete damnation. The new idea however did take root in the young intellectual circles of Peiping, Tientsin, Shanghai, Canton and other university centres. Within the next few years several other serious amateur modern theatre groups were formed in these places while one or two of the 'tea-houses' and professional theatres and 'Coney Island' entertainment centres of the type of the 'New World' in Shanghai or Peiping exploited the novelty of 'Western' staging with 'thrillers' or 'shockers'.

47

Though none of the modern plays written at that time show a serious grasp of modern dramatic technique, they do show that they were inspired by an earnest desire for social reform and intended to make the theatre serve progressive aims while exploring new artistic forms.

China's modern students have always been in the van of the revolution. The students of the first modern universities came mainly from families of the rising young Chinese bourgeoisie, middle class groups engaged in industry, commerce or the professions, or from landed aristocratic families who were investing their wealth in urban occupations. Such students were naturally attracted to the Western ideas of a realistic drama as opposed to the mythological and dynastic drama of the traditional classical stage. This was a natural corollary of their attempts to master modern Western science and industrial business methods as opposed to the unscientific thought of old China and its handicraft-peasant economy. Just as in politics, the rising young Chinese bourgeoisie opposed the feudal autocratic monarchy and demanded a democratic republic like its Western counterparts, so, in the field of the theatre (though this cultural revolution came subsequent to the political revolution in 1911), it opposed the feudal, Confucian outlook of the classical theatre and strove to develop its *own* theatre. Just as it sought to learn and copy the Western nations in the field of industry and commerce so it sought to learn from, and copy them, in the field of art. But whereas it was a comparatively simple matter to import a steam turbine and make it work in China, drama was a different matter. Plays that were effective propaganda for good progressive bourgoise ideas in Britain and America, were found to appeal only to a small coterie of Westernised intellectuals in China. It was necessary to develop a modern Chinese repertoire. This is what societies like the *Spring Willow* tried to do, with varying degrees of success.

Dr. Hu Shih, Professor Soong Tsung-fang and other bourgeois

eroine in 'Tsai Ting-hua' by Wu
wang. A Shanghai production of 1937

A Manchu Prince in 'Tsai Ting-hua'

A play of student life produced by the Lu Hsun Art Academy in Yenan,
1941, in the modern 'Western style'.

Two Yanko players in a Shensi Province village.

intellectuals in Peiping's new modern universities did the spade work of the Literary Revolution. China's classical plays and *belles lettres* up to this time were all written in the *Wen Li* style, the literary language, the language of the literati, the scholars. In its finer forms it was quite incomprehensible to the ordinary public. To the Chinese man-in-the-street it was often as incomprehensible as the scholiasts' Latin was to the man-in-the-street of the European Middle Ages. If a popular, democratic modern literature was to be written therefore, the first task was to forge a new literary medium out of the ordinary spoken language—the *Pai Hua*. While the scholars of the Literary Revolution were doing this they were also making earnest efforts to propagandise the wholesale reform of the theatre. They demanded that music and drama should be separated, as in the West, that the Aristotelian unities of space, time and action should be observed, that realistic presentation of life should take the place of the idealistic moralities of the classical theatre, that there should be actresses as well as actors on the stage, that the theatre building itself should conform to the European pattern, and that the conventions of the classical stage should be exchanged for the conventions of the Western 'picture-frame' stage.

The aims of the innovators, however, far outstripped their achievements. Some, seeing the difficulties of getting the mass audience of the common people to break sharply with the old ways, tried a more oblique approach. They sifted through the old classical repertoire, disregarded the plays based on superstition or respect for the imperial house and revived the plays that contain strong moral and revolutionary implications, plays that satirise the corrupt mandarins, denounce the tyrants and that laud the simple virtues of the common man. Some of these experimental theatre groups were endowed by public-spirited rich patrons from among the modern businessmen.

It must be remembered that throughout this period, from 1911

D

to the present, an active revolutionary struggle has been waged that sometimes simmered in one or two provinces and sometimes flared up on a nation-wide scale. As early as 1917 many student groups developed a vivid and increasingly popular theatre of the revolution, based on the Western style. They did not attempt 'big drama'. They were content to present short sketches and 'living newspapers'. Some were club theatricals but many were travelling troupes that performed in temples and fair grounds and in 'one night stands' just as did the classical theatre troupes. Their playlets dealt in simple terms with such evils as opium smoking, foot binding for women, corruption of officials and cowardice in face of foreign aggressors. During the agitation against the growing Japanese aggression, the plays showed the results of Japanese rule in Korea with the implied warning that a similar fate lay in store for China unless the people and its leaders showed greater patriotism and staunchness and self-sacrifice for the common good. They were direct, hard-hitting and did not hesitate to enlist *Grand Guignol* effects to drive home their points. One play had realistic scenes of Japanese torture—pulling out of nails, beatings and executions. Not infrequently, as in the clowning interludes of the classical theatre, local evil-doers and traitors—sellers of Japanese goods—would be pilloried by means of the stage. These developments not only spread a knowledge of the realistic drama among an ever growing audience in town and country, but prepared the actors and dramatists and other theatre workers for the very considerable achievements of the modern Western style theatre between 1931—the date of the Japanese invasion of Manchuria, and 1937, the date of the full scale Japanese invasion of all China and the national resistance of the Chinese people.

During this time the intellectuals of the big university cities developed a mature taste in Western drama. Ibsen had a particularly strong influence on all of them. His *Doll's House* especially has attracted constant attention. Next in importance has been

Anton Chekhov and Ostrovsky. The latter's *Inspector-General* is a perennially popular production with the students and public. Its rapier thrusts at grasping officials—the traditional butt of Chinese comedy—have given it all the attraction of forbidden fruit. Under the Kuomintang dictatorship playwrights did not dare to make direct attacks on bad officials. When the *Inspector-General* was produced however, everyone in the audience knew that the play really referred to the notoriously corrupt Kuomintang bureaucrats.

Only Eugene O'Neill and Bernard Shaw among Anglo-American playwrights have any considerable influence on Chinese dramatists. Very few students returned from Western countries have, in fact, made any serious contribution to dramatic literature. All the most significant creative work has been the product of Chinese who have studied only in China or only partly in Europe, though all the successful dramatists have a good knowledge of nineteenth century French, German, Russian and English literature in translation. Modern Soviet plays are well known.

The most influential of the playwrights in the modern Western style, and perhaps the most accomplished in point of technique and mastery of Western dramatic form, is Tsao Yu. His *Thunder and Rain* is the story of the breakdown of the old feudal family relations in modern times, a poignant drama of incest. *Sunrise* is a drama of contemporary Shanghai, the tragedy of the Big City.

Yuen Ching is another of the outstanding moderns. His *Under the Eaves of Chungking* is a mature production both in form and content. Hsia Yen, whose *Tears of the Yangtze* has been voted the best Chinese film to date, and Wu Tsu-kwang, are more indigenous as writers. Wu's *Tsai Ting-hua* presents the famous Peiping prostitute who mediated with the foreign invaders after the Boxer Rebellion. When it was first produced in Shanghai in 1937 it caused a sensation, though this was perhaps less due to its intrinsic merit than to the fact that by innuendo and symbolism, the playwright succeeded in outwitting the Kuomintang censors and castigated the spineless officials who were willing to submit to the Japanese invasion just as the official villains in the play were willing to submit to the foreign invaders of that time.

My personal opinion, shared by most of the leading critics, is that these plays are mature creations that will live on for many years as good, though not great, plays of their time. They show a knowledge and feeling for modern life and use the *pai hua* with a literary skill that make the efforts of Hu Shih and his colleagues in the 1920's seem adolescent. In fact the development of the new *pai hua* literature passed out of the hands of Hu Shih and his group—who linked themselves with the Chiang dictatorship—into those of the young writers who followed Lu Hsun, leader of the revolutionary wing of the Literary Renaissance. Lu Hsun, not only showed how to write in *pai hua* but taught and encouraged writers, poets, dramatists, journalists and painters and woodcut artists in the revolutionary use of the new literary idiom. Incurably ill though he was, he contained his leadership at a time when scores of progressive intellectuals were being arrested, jailed or shot out of hand by the dictatorship. The central art school of the Communist-led Liberated Areas was dedicated to him. It created the most virile productions in the Western style drama and used this form most effectively for Resistance Propaganda during the Japanese invasion. This school and its various Front Service Corps were tireless innovators. It was in Yenan that in 1938 I saw the first modern Chinese opera on a modern theme—the creation of a guerilla unit in occupied territory—in which the words were in *pai hua* and the music and general unfolding of the action were in Western form.

Thus by the early 1940's the Western style theatre had a small repertoire of Chinese plays of consequence. It also had a larger number of good translations from the foreign theatre. Actors and producers have shown a remarkable talent in the Western genres.

Productions of Shakespeare, Molière, Gogol, Ostrovsky or Ibsen are comparable to the finest in the West. Up to the outbreak of the Japanese invasion in 1937, however, the Western style theatre remained almost wholly an urban form of entertainment, and even there it was limited still to the intellectuals and small upper middle class groups.

During the period of the Japanese invasion, however, the Western style groups developed their activities on a considerable scale to reinforce the defence propaganda work of all other cultural groups. This was particularly the case during the early period of the war when all the political parties were united in a national front against the invader. In 1940, the third year of the war, there were as many as 2,500 dramatic propaganda groups with a total of 60,000 members—actors, playwrights, musicians, artists, producers. They were organised by the veteran writer Kuo Mo-jo, and by Tien Han, a nationally known figure in the world of the theatre. Most of these groups were attached to various army units and lived on soldiers' pay with the honorary ranks of majors or sergeants. Performances usually included concert turns, sketches and full length plays. In some ways this was a time of dramatic growth though there was little time for serious dramatic quests. The people in their tens of thousands were brought a first-hand knowledge of new art forms, and the intellectuals were brought into closer contact with the people than ever before. Scholars learnt to appreciate anew the riches of folk art—the ballad, the song, the recitation and the dance. Many incorporated their finds in sketches, plays and musical and dance compositions. The intellectuals and the theatre emerged from the war spiritually enriched.

The Western style drama has come to stay in China. It is a product of middle class Chinese urban culture and that culture will only develop to the full in the coming period. Hitherto the progressive middle class theatre has had more than ordinary difficulties to contend with. First it had to make its way against the complete theatrical monopoly of the imperial feudal culture and its classical theatre. Then, when the last dynasty was overthrown in 1911, it had to battle in an unequal struggle not only against the ideological resistance of the old culture, but against the persecution of the new dictatorship of Chiang Kai-shek and his allied war lords and fascist groups which used every means at their command to combat democratic and progressive ideas. This resulted in severe pressure against the modern Western style theatre for, as I have already suggested in discussing the classical theatre, Chinese cultural tradition has always regarded the theatre not only as a place of entertainment, but primarily as a place of instruction. Thus there has never been any serious argument in Chinese intellectual circles about the necessity or even the desirability of 'art for art's sake'. As Hsia Yen, one of the four leading contemporary dramatists, writes: 'The overwhelming majority of modern Chinese dramatists have consciously used their plays as a means to advance social reform'.

In the present phase of the political and social revolution that is taking place in China, the peasant and the middle classes are freeing themselves politically and economically from the old feudal system and from the shackles that have been riveted on them by the small group of big business monopolists gathered around Chiang Kai-shek. Success in this revolution which by an historic 'paradox' is led by the Chinese working class, and which now seems to be a matter of the near future, will present a full and favourable opportunity for the development of a progressive Chinese middle class culture, just as it will present the middle classes with a broad opportunity to develop trade and industry. This presages a rapid and widespread development of the Western style theatre—both progressive middle-class and proletarian—in China.

CHAPTER THREE

THE
YANGKO
THEATRE

A STUDY OF THE Chinese Yangko Theatre is a study of the development of a modern theatrical art form out of a primitive folk art within the space of the last few years. In 1938—ten years ago—Yangko dancing was a folk art curiosity in North-west China's Shensi Province. Today it has spread in its modern form of Yangko drama dealing with the most complex contemporary subjects, all over North and North-east China. In the wake of the revolutionary People's Armies it is conquering the imaginations of the people of Central China. In parts of Shensi—notably the famous Yenan Border Region on the verges of Shensi, Kansu and Ninghsia—one out of every twelve people enjoy the pleasures of a Yangko dance as a regular feature of their life.

Shensi Province is bounded by the great U-shaped bend of the Yellow River. It is one of the cradles of Chinese civilisation and therefore one of the sources of the classical Chinese theatre. Down to this day you can find here survivals of the primitive folk rituals from which the classical theatre sprang. Such a survival is the original Yangko. It is a folk song and dance performed at the time of field labour; a fertility rite danced by youths and maidens. As performed in the recent past it was a group dance with some twenty or thirty dancers to a group. The leader held an open umbrella or a metal rod and he sang the theme of the play while the chorus chanted in answer. Male and female dancers faced each other in opposite lines. In later days, however, the female parts were, as in the classical theatre, played by boys. The songs are mostly in the form of questions and answers between the men and women, love themes or congratulatory addresses. The basic dance movement is a vigorous advance of three steps forward followed by one swinging step backwards and sideways. This movement sets the rhythm for entrance and exit of the troupe. In between, there are many variations of rhythm, step and gesture corresponding to the characters the dancers personify, but usually, as befits the central theme of the rite, the swaying, swinging movements are suggestive of sex.

Two Yangko Dancers

I had always thought that the mincing steps, the paper umbrellas and fans, the peculiar way in which ballerinas of the classical Western ballet in 'Chinese transformation scenes' dance with the index finger of both hands pointing upwards before them, was entirely make-believe 'Chinoiserie', but I found that this style of representing Chinese dancing is quite authentic. These are the very steps and gestures that one sees in Shensi Yangko dancing.

In addition to the solos of the principal characters there are group movements in which the lines of the dancers weave fanciful patterns on the ground to the accompaniment of the rhythmic beats of the drums, the gongs, the punctuating or exciting clash of the cymbals and the melodious line of the *Hu Ch'in* violin. Commentators note that the leading musical role was played by the percussion. The strings and wind instruments are a later addition. Not infrequently a clown appeared as a separate character. It is abundantly clear that Yangko was essentially an out-of-doors spectacle since it was of two main types: 'A story on the ground' performed on foot, or, 'a story on horseback', in which latter case the theme of the dance drama was usually an heroic historical one like the famous combat between the General Lu Pu of the Han dynasty (206 B.C.) and the Three Heroes.

Such was Yangko when the Communist-led People's Armies first arrived in Shensi Province in 1934.

It was in 1937, at the start of the full-scale struggle against the Japanese invasion, that the local Communist propaganda groups began to make creative use of the ancient Yangko traditions. In the first typical new Yangko, the leader, instead of an umbrella, carried a rifle or a farming tool or other symbol and the line of dancers or chorus, instead of acting like men and women courting, dressed themselves as farmers, students, workers, soldiers or merchants and represented the people of all classes united in the struggle against the invader. The new theme songs expressed various new social and political ideas. The clown was now often dressed like a Japanese or a quisling. Yet, few intellectuals even then thought of Yangko as an art with great possibilities, though the new Yangko became more and more popular among the peasants. It was in fact a farmer, Liu Chi-jen of the Yenan Region who further developed the new Yangko in 1937, by incorporating a short dramatic action as an extension of the theme song and dance. Liu Chi-jen's group produced Yangko dance dramas whose names are self-explanatory: 'Public Food Reserves for

National Salvation', 'The People's Defence Corps on Guard'. Yangko now took hold of the popular imagination as it had never before done when it was merely a seasonal fertility rite rooted in mystical superstition.

Yangko evenings were more and more frequently arranged in villages, in market towns, in school yards or village meeting-halls. First, the clangorous instruments summon the people with their vigorous dance rhythm in typical and unmistakably Yangko style. The expectant crowd forms a big open circle. The leaders set the theme of the spectacle in a ballad and the chorus, dressed as farmers, follows them in the opening dance. Three steps forward, a sweeping sidestep back. Soon the 'audience' too joins in the general round dance. There is all the merriment of a village fête the world over as the young entice the oldsters to unloosen their feet, forget their dignity for the moment and join in the dance. At Yangko evenings in Yenan I have seen the leading officials of the government and the Communist Party dragged into the laughing circle, though General Chu Teh, Commander-in-Chief of the People's Armies, never needs a second invitation. Finally, the music reaches a climax of speed and drum beats. Inside the circle that is then formed by the public, the leaders perform a simple play in song and verse, dialogue and dance. A young brother and sister are turning up virgin soil to help increase production for the national war effort. The brother teases his sister by pretending to be lazy. The girl gets very indignant and tries to persuade him to reform. She uses all the well-tried arguments of the propagandists, but the boy seems to take no notice at all, till with a great laugh he gives up the joke just as his sister is reduced to tears. The happy ending leads to general rejoicing and merrymaking. The chorus starts the round dance till once again it becomes general. Often two or three plays will follow in quick succession.

'The villains', writes Guenther Stein in his *Challenge of Red*

A Shensi "Yangko" Melody

Theme in "Brother and Sister Cultivating Virgin Soil"

China, 'are either Japanese soldiers and Chinese traitors or witch doctors, loafers and other anti-social elements who hamper the war effort, the increase of production, or the march of political and social progress. The heroes and heroines are Eighth Route Army (People's Army) soldiers, militiamen, or simple pioneers of class unity and mutual aid; fighters against superstition, illiteracy, dirt and disease; or model workers in villages, factories, co-operatives and government offices whose individual action has aroused the initiative of the masses.'

By 1944, at the height of the struggle against the Japanese invasion, the intellectuals in these Communist-led areas of the great Resistance Movement became convinced that hitherto they had circumscribed their activities too much within their own intimate circles and interests, that to broaden their outlook and the scope of their work they must, as Chou Erh-fu, who has himself produced several successful Yangko, writes, 'really grasp the spirit and feelings of the Chinese people, go out to the villages and live with them, learn their language, how they express their feelings in their own art. Encouraged by talks with Mao Tze-tung, the Communist Party leader, it was then that the intellectuals joined in the Yangko activities with a new zest and injected fresh inspiration into this newest art form. 'They discarded their former prejudice against Yangko as 'lowbrow' entertainment or as a remnant of feudal art that in itself bore poisonous elements of feudal ideas, superstition and sexuality. They ceased their literary attacks on Yangko, and became its most sympathetic supporters and enthusiastic participants!'

Yangko began to develop along more complex lines as the two streams of culture from the peasants and the modern intellectuals met and joined. Today, some performances like that of the *White Haired Woman* and *Chou Tsi-shan* last for four or five hours, with many scenes and with an action spread over many years. In some of the more elaborate performances produced on stages by the students of the Liberated Area Universities, one can trace the influence of the classical theatre and also of the Western theatre of the most advanced type. In their acting of certain types they adapt many of the 'gesture patterns' of the classical theatre.

Thus a new theatrical form has arisen that is remarkable for its great vitality and potentialities. It stands close to the springs of national art. Through the intellectuals it is able to draw on all the accumulated stores of cultural wealth of both China and the West. It has spread rapidly throughout the Liberated Areas that have been freed from the Chiang Kai-shek dictatorship and advances as the popular revolution advances, taking on ever new aspects as it is enriched by the inspiration of various, more local, cultures.

In many villages of these regions Yangko has become a regular weekly event. One of the *Ten Small Points* that the People's Government has widely proclaimed and encouraged for the improvement of village life, calls for the establishment of at least one Yangko group in every community. Guenther Stein in his book on the new China writes: 'The Chinese country and small town folk love entertainment and are starved for it. The Yangko has acted on them like rain on parched earth. It has brought them not only theatre, but theatre they can easily understand. For it deals with matters close to their own lives—instead of putting before them the kings, queens, and concubines, the feudal warriors, courtiers, ghosts, and jesters which dominated their ancestors' imaginations in ages long gone by when Chinese art became formal and stagnant.'

Nothing can remain static in the marvellous epoch of change that China has entered upon, and least of all the Theatre—that synthesis of all the imaginative arts. Classical Style Theatre, Western Style Theatre and Yangko will all, that is certain, have great new developments to show even while this book is being printed, so we will attempt no final judgement.

BIBLIOGRAPHY

The Chinese Drama by R. F. Johnson
      Kelly and Walsh, Shanghai, 1921.

The Chinese Theatre by A. E. Zucker
      Jarrolds, London, 1925

Secrets of the Chinese Drama by Cecilia S. L. Zung
      George G. Harrup Ltd., London, 1937

The Chinese Theatre by A. Jacovleff and Tchou Kia-kien
      John Lane, The Bodley Head, London, 1922

The Challenge of Red China by Guenther Stein
      Pilot Press, London, 1945.

This book is set in 12pt. Fournier, a letter based on the original design by Pierre Simon Fournier. Fournier was the first of many famous type-designers of the eighteenth century to cut complete families of types, large-faced and small-faced romans, condensed and bold faces. The invention of the point-system of type-measurement is ascribed to him.

The Monotype version used in this book is based on one of Fournier's medium text-types, and is one of the narrowest book-faces available today. The accompanying italic version is a graceful letter differing in its fundamental conception from other italic types.

Typography by Henry Jacob, M.S.I.A.